A SWEET THING

Barbara Gross

Copyright © 2023 by Barbara Gross

All rights reserved.

No portion of this book may be reproduced in any form without written permission from the publisher or author, except as permitted by U.S. copyright law.

contents

(1) Meet James "Jammy" Barnes — 1

(2) Meet McKenna Taylor Harlow — 4

(3) Present Day — 8

(4) The Day They Met — 13

(5) My Usual — 18

(6) Wanted to See You — 21

(7) Drinks With The Guys — 24

(8) Rekindling The Flame — 27

(9) Dancing In The Kitchen — 31

(10) Sam's Birthday — 37

(11) Sushi Wine & Dine — 41

(12) Aspen Romance — 44

(13) Celebrations & Truths Unraveled — 50

(14) The Unraveling — 54

(15) Moving Out & On — 60

(16) Breaking News!! — 63

(17) Discussions, Divorce and Denials — 67

(18) I'm All Yours — 74

(19) Slap Fest — 77

(20) Meeting The Family — 81

(21) McKenna's Surprise Party — 85

(22) The New Mrs Barnes — 88

(23) Cayman Islands — 92

(24) Meet Henry James Barnes — 94

Epilogue — 96

(1) Meet James "Jammy" Barnes

Four years ago,

"Do you James take Shayla to be your lawful wedded wife forsaking all others as long as you both shall live?" A minister said

"I do." He said

"And do you Shayla take James to be your lawful wedded husband forsaking all others as long as you both shall live?" A minister said

"I do." She said

"Without any further a do I now pronounce you husband and wife. Mr Barnes you may now kiss your bride." A minister said

Jammy kissed Shayla his long time sweetheart since senior year of highschool. They were now 27 years old. She wanted them to get married after they were done with school. That included when he was done with business school.

At the reception James came over to the newly weds. "What's this I hear that you started up your own business. You are a Barnes." James said

Jammy just walked away. "Who are you?" Shayla asked

"I'm James Barnes III your father in law. Despite what my son thinks of Marcus I am his father." James said as he handed her his business card.

"You wouldn't happen to be looking for a assistant. My degree is in business personal assistant. I've just been his receptionist for the last year." She said

"As a matter of fact I am. The one I had quit two weeks ago and I've waiting for the right one to come through. Can you come in on Monday for a interview?" He said

"Yes I can." She said

"Great come around 2." James said as he walked away.

James found his ex wife. "Why did you let him start up his own company?" James said

"Same reason he no longer wants to be around you." Winnie said as she cut him a cold hard stare.

James shook his head and walked away.

****

"What do you mean you quit?" Jammy said

"I had a job interview with your father this afternoon. He offered me a job James. I can use my degree." Shayla said

"Shay baby no. Call him back and tell him you changed your mind. That man is the devil he's a horrible mean person! You can't work for him!" He yelled

"James! That is your father the person who helped give life to you. I didn't even know he existed till three days ago. I didn't waste my time in college to let my degree collect dust while I'm sitting at a desk at your office answering the phone!" Shayla said

Jammy rolled his eyes and walked out. He ended up going to one of his best friends place to cool off and crashed there. Three days into their marriage and already had a huge fight.

(2) Meet McKenna Taylor Harlow

Also four years ago

Somewhere else in NY, McKenna Harlow was graduating from Culinary school. Everything in her life was perfect. She and her high-school sweetheart Braylon had been engaged for six months and was about to leave for Boston so he could attend law school.

A week after her graduation she was starting to pack. When her older brother Gabe called her.

"Sis, I heard to Brooklyn Med now. It's dad." Gabe said

"Dad? What about dad?" She said

"Coby called he said dad collapsed and was gasping for air." Gabe said

"I'll meet you there. Gracie in school." She said

"Yeah she is." Gabe said

McKenna hung up the phone and bolted. She met Gabe and her sister in law who was 6 months pregnant. Gabe was pacing while McKenna bounced her legs and chewed her lip.

"I'm looking for Mr Bryant Harlow's family." A doctor said

"That's us. It's just me and my sister and my wife. I'm his son." Gabe said

"I wish I had better news. You two need to discuss what your father's wishes were. He suffered a massive stroke. We haven't had any brain activity in the last hour. We have done everything we could Mr Harlow and Ms Harlow." The doctor said

Mckenna sat down and began to cry. "Um I know what his wishes are. But we have one more person that needs to be here. Our baby sister she's 16. I'm gonna go get her so she can say her goodbyes too." Gabe said

"Okay. We will wait." The doctor said

"Thank you." Gabe said as he tried to hold back the tears.

"Stay with her darlin. I'll be back." Gabe said to his wife.

"Okay." She said as she rubbed McKenna's back.

Forty five minutes later Gabe returned with Gracelynn who had tears. They all four went into the room Bryant was in. They said their goodbyes and told him them how much they loved him. To tell mom hi for them.

They held hands as they turned off the machines. A few days later the same day as Jammy's wedding was their dad's funeral.

That Monday Gabe and McKenna met with their dad's lawyer.

"Okay in the matter of your younger sister. Because she is still considered a minor she is left in the care of McKenna. The bakery is also left to McKenna. The estate is being split three ways the house goes to Gabe. The apartment above the bakery goes to McKenna since she now owns the bakery. Your grandmother's house that your parents took ownership over it says here that you three can decide what to do. So here is all the legal paperwork that shows ownership and guardianship of Gracelynn." The lawyer said

"Thank you Mr Compton." Gabe said

They left the office and had lunch as they discussed everything. When McKenna returned to her apartment.

"So I'm going on to Boston to get the apartment ready. While you deal with everything when you are done you can come on." Braylon said

"I can't go." She said

"What?" He said

"I'm Gracelynn's legal guardian and I have ownership of the family bakery I can't go." She said

"Just move Grace with us. She can transferred schools and that bakery can be closed down. You can open a new one." Braylon said

"Excuse me! No i will not up root my life and my sister's life for you!" She said

"We have already put in our notice Kenna and I put a deposit down on the new place! This has been our plan!" Braylon said

"Well I'm sorry that my dad dying was such inconvenience for you! But I'm not going to Boston my family needs me here! So here take this back and go to Boston without me. Have a nice life Bray." She said as she threw her ring at him and opened the door for him.

"Whatever McKenna." Braylon said and walked out.

Gracelynn and McKenna moved into the apartment above the bakery. She gave her sister the bedroom and she slept on the pull out couch Gabe gave them that was at their dad's house.

(3) Present Day

"Where are you going?" Jammy said as he wrapped his arms around Shayla from behind.

"Not now James. I have a flight to catch in an hour." Shayla said

"But Shay doll." He said

"I said not now. I'm busy I have to finish packing and leave to meet your father. We have a business trip in Tokyo." She said

"Why is it always you that he needs to take? He has other people at that gigiantic ass building." Jammy said

"Maybe because I'm the only one that knows how to close a deal." She said as she slammed her suitcase lid.

"But Shayla today is.." he said but was cut off.

"I don't care that you had a bad day." She said and left.

"It's our anniversary Shay." He whispered as he looked down.

He cancelled their dinner reservations and left the gift bag on her vanity in the closet. Meanwhile across the street from his penthouse was Harlow Bakery. McKenna was working on a wedding cake when her brother came in with his wife and their 4 year old daughter Rayna.

"Auntie Kenna!" Rayna said as she tugged on McKenna's apron.

McKenna pulled out the air pods she had in. "Hey Gabe Raegan and Rayna.." she said

"Harlow Bakery had a face lift and was brought back to life." Gabe said as he held up the Brooklyn Tribune.

She rolled her eyes as she walked away.

"Rayna was you good at preschool today?" As she opened up a container

"I was very good today. I counted to 5 auntie Kenna." Rayna said as she held up one of her hands.

McKenna held a cupcake with pink frosting and purple sprinkles behind her back. She squatted down to her niece.

"You counted to 5. Show me?" She said

Rayna started to count five fingers. "Good job now I want you to close your eyes. Hold out that hand of five fingers." McKenna said

Rayna held out her hand and closed her eyes tightly. McKenna placed the cupcake in her little niece's hand.

"Open." McKenna said

Rayna gasped when she saw her cupcake. "Auntie Kenna knows magic daddy." Rayna said

"Why don't you and mommy go out there and eat that magical cupcake while I talk to auntie Kenna." Gabe said as he picked her up and gave her a kiss.

Raegan and Rayna left the kitchen.

"You really have turned this place around Mac." Gabe said as she sat up on the counter top.

She looked down.

"They would be so proud not just mom and dad but all of our family generations that has worked so hard in this kitchen running this business." Gabe said as he nudged her.

"Yeah." She said

"And you managed to do it all while taking care of Gracie. And look at her now she's a sophomore in college." Gabe said

"How's your fellowship going?" She said

"It's going good. Dealing with brains all day is so much fun." He said

She let out a laugh.

"Order pick up for Winnie Barnes? Where is the box?" Charlotte said

"The pink one Charly it's the one that says W. Barnes." McKenna said as she hopped off the counter.

Gabe hugged her. "We will get out of your hair. I just wanted to talk to you." Gabe said

"It's always nice when you visit." She said as he left.

She put her AirPods back in and began to finish the cake. Jammy showed up at his mom's who was making dinner.

"Hey mom." He said

"Oh hey honey. I didn't expect to see you tonight. You didn't have to be here for Ruthie's birthday dinner I know it's your.." Winnie said but as she turned around she stopped.

"What's wrong?" She said

"She's on another trip she acted like she didn't even know what today was." He said as he shoved a mouth full of stuffed mushrooms in his mouth.

Winnie sighed and hugged him. "It'll be okay. Everyone else should be here soon." She said as she went back to the stove.

(4) The Day They Met

Two months later

Jammy walked into Harlow Bakery like he does every morning to pick up coffee and normally he gets just donuts for himself on his way to work. But they were meeting a potential client and so Sam ordered donuts from the bakery.

"Hi I'm Makayla can I help you?" Makayla said

"Yes. A coffee to go and I also have to pick up a donut order. It's under BRW contracting and Engineering." Jammy said

Charlotte walked by with muffins to put on display. "Good morning Mr Barnes." Charlotte said

"Good morning Charlotte." He said as Makayla came over with all the coffee Sam ordered and a pink box that said Harlow Bakery on it.

He opened it up to see the order was all wrong. Instead of just normal glazed donuts they were all colored and sprinkled.

"Wait, my colleague who placed the order specifically asked for plain glazed donuts." He said

Charlotte heard him as she continued to put the muffins out. "I have a meeting in an hour! And I needed these for that meeting! And I can't go in there with these!" He snapped

Charlotte came over with the order form. "Makayla..how could you not ask if they want colors." Charlotte said

"Charlotte I want to speak to the manager." Jammy said

Charlotte went to the back as McKenna took off her apron. "I heard him." She said as she walked out.

Jammy was pacing but had his back to her as she came out.

"Hi I'm McKenna Harlow the manager/owner. What happened?" She said

Jammy turned around and felt his heart skipped a beat. McKenna's breathe hitched as she swallowed hard.

Jammy swallowed hard. "My donuts are wrong. I asked for plain glazed.." he said

McKenna opened the box and read the order form that Charlotte handed her.

"Charlotte make sure the coffee is correct. Makayla wait in my office." McKenna said as she picked up the box.

Makayla wiped her face and went to the back. "I'll fix this Mr Barnes." She said as she went to the back.

She put fresh baked donuts in a new box and came back out. "Everything else correct Charlotte." She said

"Yes ma'am." Charlotte said

"It's on the house Mr Barnes. And I promise it won't happen again." She said as she put creamers and sugars in a bag.

"Thank you Ms Harlow." He said

She smiled at him. "Welcome. Enjoy the rest of your day Mr Barnes." She said

But as she was about to go back to deal with Makayla she saw his wedding ring.

"Enjoy the rest of your day Ms Harlow." He said as he left.

She caught her breathe as she walked into the kitchen. "To bad.." she thought

"Makayla!" McKenna said

She came out of the office wiping tears. "Stop crying. Don't ever let that happen again! Do you know who that is? That is Mr Barnes..Barnes around here means something. His family are loyal customers around here. For generations the Barnes have used this bakery. They have their own section in the order book. And you just screwed up the order. You are lucky I had just finished a fresh batch of glazed donuts." She said

Makayla kept her head down.

"Charlotte!" McKenna said

Charlotte came into the kitchen. "Yes ma'am." She said

"Train her on orders again. Make sure she understands that she needs to ask if the customer wants colors." McKenna said as she went back to making all the breakfast items.

That night Jammy was alone since Shayla was gone again. Jammy was laying in his bed as he stared at his ceiling. He began to think about McKenna and her gorgeous smile and dimples.

"Mmm McKenna.." he whispered as he began to jerk.

Across the street in the apartment above the bakery. McKenna was in the tub as she began to play with herself. As her orgasm came crashing over her she moaned out "James."

"Who ever she is, is one lucky woman." She thought to herself.

She turned off the lights after she got out and went to bed. Jammy was able to finish and went to sleep too.

(5) My Usual

The next morning when he came in he saw McKenna. She looked up when she heard the bell.

"You came back?" She said with a smile.

"I did. I wasn't going to stop coming. I wasn't that angry." He said

"Your usual?" She said

"Yes please." He said

She went to make his coffee she mixed it and sat it on the counter. He turned his head to the side as she bent over to get donuts. He felt a twitch in his pants and let out a small groan. She came back over to the counter.

Jammy swallowed hard. "You're very beautiful Ms Harlow." He said

She smiled. "Thank you." She said

"You're welcome. But your mom was beautiful too. I remember coming in here when I was younger with my mom." He said

McKenna looked down. "She was. You have a great day Mr Barnes." She said as she gave him his receipt.

"You have a great day too Ms Harlow." He said with a wink and left.

He left and she could finally breathe again. "He's married he's married he's just being friendly Kenna." She thought to herself.

Jammy was all smiles as he drove to work. Later that day he stopped by to see her again as she was started her closing stuff.

"You know it's not morning." She said

"I wanted to see you." He said

He was leaning on the counter she came over to him. She placed her hand on his and ran her thumb on his wedding band.

"You're married James." She whispered

"I know that. But since yesterday I haven't stopped thinking about you." He whispered

"You need to stop. I'm not the type of girl that will be the mistress." She whispered

He caressed her cheek and tucked some blonde hair behind her ear.

"McKenna, please let me have you." He whispered as he ran a thumb along her bottom lip.

"James I can't..I can't be..that girl." She whispered as she tried so hard to fight the urge.

"I'm not gonna give up.." he whispered as he rested his forehead against hers.

"You should.." she whispered as he kissed her cheek.

"Never.." he said as he left her there.

(6) wanted to see you

Two weeks later

Jammy had been coming by for the last two weeks after work to eat pie. It was a Tuesday morning Jammy had already been by to get his usual. But they were having a last minute meeting and he wanted to have donuts and coffee.

So he called the bakery McKenna took the phone call when Makayla asked about delivery.

"James.." she said

"I need a dozen donuts and a dozen muffins. And about 8 coffees." He said

"But we don't.." she said

"I know you don't but nobody has to know." He said

She looked down.

"I'll pay you extra for the gas." He said

"Fine.." she said

McKenna put together the order when Gracie came in. "We don't do delivery unless it's a wedding." She said

"Shut up Gracie. I'll be back." She said and she left.

She made her way to the city and to Jammy's office building. When she made her way upstairs he met her at the elevator.

He smiled at her. She followed him to the conference room and she sat everything down. He paid her in cash.

She was about to leave when he stopped her. "What?" She said

"You look so cute all flustered." He said

"I'm not flustered. I'm irritated that you made me drive all the way out here." She said

"Well your bakery is the only bakery I trust." He said

"Well that's good news." She said

"And I wanted to see you again." He said as he caressed her cheek.

"James we talked about this." She whispered

"You talked.." he whispered in her ear.

They left the conference room and went into his office.

"And it clearly went in one ear out the other." She said

"I can't help that you make me feel things and think such dirty things about you." He whispered

Jammy went to lean down to kiss her but got her cheek. "James.." she whispered

"McKenna.." he whispered as she left.

"Hey McKenna thanks for the donuts." Sam said

"Oh hey Sam and Steve good morning." She said as she left.

Jammy sat down in his desk chair and groaned.

(7) Drinks with the Guys

^ Jammy's step brothers Jiovanni and Malcolm. Sam, Lucas, Steve, Scott, Clint and Pietro. ^

Four nights later

Jammy joined his friends and stepbrothers at a cigar bar in Brooklyn.

"You are being quiet again. Are you okay?" Steve said

Lucas looked up at Jammy and gave him a look. Jammy shook his head no as he spun his glass when he seen Lucas' look.

"Me and Shay are just having some problems. I knew that her working for the devil would be bad. Just didn't think it would be this bad. He always needs her on trips, hell he just took her to Tokyo on our anniversary. She didn't even care she forgot about it. I had dinner reservations and a gift." He said

"Damn.." Sam said

"Yeah. She avoids baby talk..I honestly don't know what happened. This isn't how we pictures married life or not how I pictured it anyways. Me feeling alone in my own marriage." He said

"I know my brother in law has said in the past that "the devil" can be pushy at times and can be a dick. But to be that way with his own daughter in law is fucking bull shit." Lucas said

Jammy gave him a look. "I know that you don't like me saying that. But she is his daughter in law regardless." Lucas said

"You know what dad would say." Jio said

"What? And please God don't let it be something that he has said he's done for mom." Jammy said

They all started laughing.

"Romance James. Try and find that fire you two once had. Make dinner bring her flowers do something to rekindle the flame." Jiovanni said

"Yeah..it's kinda hard to do that when she wants nothing to do with me. But I'll give it try again." Jammy said as they all put out their cigars and paid their tabs.

Once it was just Lucas and Jammy waiting by their cars.

"You good man?" Lucas said

"I saw that look in there. I'm not going back down that road Luke. I just wish my wife would be my wife again. Instead of being my dad's workaholic assistant." He said

"Call me if ya need me." Lucas said as they shared a hug.

"Thanks Luke. Get home safe." Jammy said

"Anytime I also have a couch if you need that too. See you at the office on Monday." Lucas said as he got into the car.

They both went their separate ways.

(8) Rekindling the Flame

The next night when she returned home she walked in to find candles lit.

"Hey darlin." Jammy said as he came to the door.

He took her stuff from her.

"James what's going on?" She said

"I'm making you dinner. Come on I have other surprises." He said as he took her hand and walked her to their master suite bathroom.

He had more candles lit and a hot rose petal filled bath ready. He gave her a glass of her favorite wine.

"You enjoy this while I go finish up dinner." He said as he kissed her forehead.

Jammy left her there in the bathroom to finish dinner. Twenty minutes later she joined him for dinner and the dessert was her favorite chocolate covered strawberries. She ate them while he gave her a neck & back massage. He also massaged her feet because she was always in heels.

When they went into the bedroom he went to kiss her and slid his hand up her thigh.

"What are you doing?" She said

"I'm trying to have sex with my wife. Because we haven't had sex in months." He said

"Jammy I'm really tired." She said

He got out of the bed, grabbed pillow and his phone.

"Where are you going?" She said

"That's always your excuse Shayla. It's either I'm to tired or I'm leaving. Or I need to sleep cause I have a red eye flight. I knew you working for that man was a bad idea but you didn't listen to me." He said as he walked out.

He went and slept in his home office. The next morning he didn't even bother going by the bakery he just went straight to work. He was slamming every door he came in contact with.

Luke and the guys was standing in the hall discussing a meeting they had scheduled that morning. When Jammy came down the hall and didn't even acknowledge them. He slammed his office door and locked it. He sat against it and fought back tears.

He finally reeled it all in and stood up as he unlocked the door.

"Susan will you get me a coffee please." He said to his secretary.

"Yes sir." She said

The guys came into his office. "Who pissed in your Cheerios?" Malcolm said

"Don't..I am in no mood." He said

"What happened between now and Saturday night?" Jiovanni said

"I took your advice..and it didn't get me no where. Everything was going great till we went to bed and tried to put the moves on her. She rejected me again..so I slept in my home office. And she had the gal to ask me why I was leaving the bedroom like she didn't know why I was pissed." He said

"Oh wow..I didn't know it was that bad." Jio said

"Here's your coffee sir." Susan said as she came in.

"Thank you Susan." He said as he took it from her.

After she shut the door back. "I feel like he's turned her against me." He said as he looked to Lucas.

"I don't think he would do something like that." Steve said

Jammy looked down. "We should get ready for the meeting." He said

While all the others left Lucas stayed. "You don't think that do you?" Lucas said

Jammy sat down in his chair and ran his hands over his face then through his hair.

"I don't know Luke. But he would do whatever he could to hurt me. But anyways make sure all the blueprints aren't messed up this time." Jammy said

"Okay. Just breathe and think about puppies. Puppies are always my go to cause it's something cute and always brings a smile to my face." He said

Jammy smirked. "Puppies Luke? Really?" Jammy said

"What it works. Sometimes I even go to the shelter. Kittens work too." He said

"Go work." Jammy said as he shook his head.

(9) Dancing in the Kitchen

Two weeks later

Jammy was at a charity ball he was standing with the guys and their wives.

"What is up with Shay?" Nat said

"I don't know..she's just been distant lately." He said as Lucas joined the group.

"Evening boys, ladies you look lovely." Lucas said

"Finally now I don't look some weirdo." Jammy said

"Dude I had to wait for my sister. She helps me with picking out my shit for these things so I don't embarrass her." Lucas said

As the night wore on it became apparent to his friends that Shayla wasn't having anything to do with Jammy. He scanned the room as another slow song began and he didn't see her anywhere. He figured she just went to the bathroom. He kept searching for her after it had been thirty minutes. She finally returned to the ballroom and got herself another drink.

When the ball was over it was quiet in the limo just like the ride to the ball. He had undid his bow tie and he looked over at her.

"Have I done something?" He said when she pushed his hand away from hers.

"Jam I'm tired okay. Geez." She said

He looked out the window as he wiped a stray tear. "You know we don't have to have sex Shayla I'd be happy with a blow job at this point. It would be nice for once in this marriage you made me feel like you want me." He said as they approached the penthouse building.

She just rolled her eyes and started to go inside. While he started to go towards the parking garage.

"Where are you going?" She said

"Not like you care." He said as he walked backwards.

When he got in his car he called McKenna's cellphone. She was working on the last wedding cake she had to make.

"Hello?" She said

"Hey it's James.." he said

"Oh you are calling me late. Haven't seen much of you lately." She said

"I'm coming over..I need to see you." He said

"James.." she whispered

"I'll be there soon. I'm not far I live across the street from the bakery." He said

He started up the car and made his way behind the bakery. He parked next to her car she let him in through the back.

"You look fancy." She said

"I had charity ball to attend." He said as he followed her inside.

She began to put the finishing touches on the cake. Once she was done she looked at him.

"I was starting to think that maybe you finally listened to me." She said

"Dance with me?" He said

She looked at him confused. "Dance with me Mckenna." He said

She took off her apron. "I don't understand what you see when you look at me." She said as she began to turn off everything and go upstairs.

He followed her upstairs as she unlocked her apartment door.

"I see beautiful woman who is smart and talented. And very stubborn." He said as he came into the apartment.

"Let me put this into perspective. You are a Barnes a well known member of society. A high ranking CEO who is married. But even if you weren't married James you could have any heiress out there. I'm just a baker.." she said as she looked down.

"I'm a mess and you are standing here in what looks to be a 4 thousand dollar tux and I'm covered in flour and you are asking me to dance." She said

Jammy slipped off the jacket and his bow tie. He undid a few buttons and his cuff links. He rolled up his sleeves as he walked towards her.

"You sound crazy right now." He said as he pulled her hair down. Her long blonde hair fell down over her shoulders.

"James." She whispered

"You are beautiful and you shouldn't think so low of yourself McKenna." He said

He caressed her cheek and ran his thumb along her bottom lip. "I'd give anything to kiss these beautiful delectable pouty lips. To hold you close to me." He said

She swallowed hard.

He hit play on his phone and laid it on her kitchen counter.

Versace on The Floor began to play as he pulled her closer and they began to dance in the middle of her small kitchen. Their foreheads together he felt her body relax into his arms.

"See not so bad." He whispered

The next song that started up was "Dreaming of You." By Cigarettes After Sex. He began to sing the words in her ear. She smiled as he did.

By the end of four songs she saw that it was after 1 in the morning.

"You should go." She whispered as he dipped her.

He pulled her back up to him and spun her. He pulled her back into his arms. "I wanna stay." He whispered in her ear.

"James.." she whispered

"I wanna hold you baby. I wanna hold you all night feel you next to me. I'll be good baby I promise." He whispered

She looked up at him. She wanted to say no but what came out was yes. They went into her bedroom she changed in her bathroom. She joined him in the bed they fell asleep nose to nose as he held her.

(10) Sam's Birthday

A week later

Jammy came into the bakery Friday afternoon.

"Hey.." he said when he met her around back.

"Hey.." she said

"So tomorrow night is Sam's birthday. His wife Milena owns a club and she's shutting it down for the night for her man. We all have the club to ourselves." He said

"Okay." She said

"I'm asking you to come, you can bring some friend preferably single ones I have two stepbrothers that are still single and my best friend is single too." He said as he held her hips.

"What about your wife?" She whispered as she ran her fingers over his band.

"She is to busy." He whispered as he made her look at him.

"Can we take a nap or just lay down?" He whispered

"I'm still working.." she whispered

"You'll still here just upstairs with me." He whispered

"Later okay.. and yes I'll go tomorrow. And I'm a single girl so of course I have single friends." She said

"Okay." He said as he went back to his car.

****

"Where's the girls you said you had invited." Lucas said

Sam came over to Jammy. "Stairs Barnes." He said

Jammy looked up. "Fuuck" he whispered

"Oh hell." Lucas said

"Hi boys. Happy Birthday Sam." She said

"Thank you McKenna." Sam said

"These are my friends "single friends" Melinda Rochelle and Alexis. And of course you all probably see these two at my bakery Charlotte and Coby are a couple." She said

Lucas couldn't take his eyes off Rochelle.

"Go play boys. Leave me with this one." Jammy said as he pulled McKenna in between his legs.

"What do you want to drink baby?" He whispered

"Vodka cranberry." She said

A few drinks in she had Jammy on the dance floor with her. They were dancing to "Miami." By Will Smith. The dance floor was filled with their friends as they all danced. All night Jammy was doing all he could to keep his need for sex in check. But having her all over him all night wasn't helping him when she looked the way she did.

"We love her Jam." Nat said as McKenna and her girls went to the bathroom.

"Okay. Thanks." Jammy said

"We just wanted you to know. That if you do end up leaving Shay we definitely approve of that one." Hope said

"Thanks." He said

That night he stayed with her while Rochelle went home with Lucas. The others exchanged phone numbers.

(11) Sushi Wine & Dine

Two nights later

Jammy showed up as she was closing up.

"Hurry up." He said

"What is the rush? My bed isn't going anywhere." She said

"I'm not wanting a nap right now. I made us reservations." He said

She looked up from counting the money. "It's 830." She said

"So..I'm taking you to dinner." He said

She bit her lip and finished counting the money. She closed down the cash registers and took the zip bag and put it in the office. He followed her upstairs so she could quickly shower and change.

"You could of warned me." She said as she came out of the bedroom.

"I wanted to surprise you." He said

They went to Tao for sushi and wine. They talked about their day and work. When they got back to her place. He held her hips and leaned down to kiss her. She began to kiss him back even though her brain was screaming that this was wrong. She felt him move down her neck.

A moan escaped her mouth as he began to suck on her sweet spot. He walked her backwards to the couch. He dropped his suit jacket on the floor when he laid her down. Moans and lip smacking began to fill the air.

He looked down as he felt unbuttoning his shirt. She began to kiss his neck he let out moan as she pushed him up and straddled him on the couch. She began to move to his chest and sucked.

"Oh baby..mmm Oh god mmm Mckenna baby.." he felt his erection getting harder with each suck.

She kissed his lips.

He looked at her. "I wanna taste you..but what I want is me in your mouth." He whispered with his lust filled blue eyes on hers.

She got up off him. "Where are you going?" He whispered

She unzipped her dress. "You coming." She said

"Yes." He said as he kicked off his shoes and followed her. They got in position he began to eat her as she sucked him. Moans began to fill the air again she loved the way his beard felt. Multiple orgasms she had even after she got him off.

She fell asleep on his chest as he fell asleep. The next morning she woke up to him staring at her.

"I never got a chance to tell you last night that you taste so sweet." He whispered as he kissed her.

"Mmm." She whispered

He gave her a wicked grin. "You're gonna have beard burn baby. I'll shav-" he said

"No..I'd be so upset if you did. I loved it." She whispered as she got up and took a shower. He joined her then left before any of the employees seen him.

(12) Aspen Romance

Three months later

It was the weekend after Christmas when Jammy whisked Mckenna off on a trip as her Christmas present. He took her to Aspen Co where his stepdad owns a chalet near a ski resort. He found her outside watching the snow fall after he got all their luggage brought in.

He slid his hands into hers. She looked down to see his band wasn't there.

He leaned down. "Don't panic, it's in my drawer at my office." He whispered

She looked up at him over her shoulder. She kissed him. "Just me and you baby." He whispered

The first couple of days they enjoyed skiing and Jammy cooked them dinner. Danced in the kitchen every night. It was New Years Eve Jammy made chocolate covered strawberries with her help. He made them a spot by the fireplace while she was in the shower.

Champagne was chilling on a table by the strawberries. He got the fireplace going when she came down stairs in a red and black silk lingerie.

"Holy fuck." He whispered

"Do you like it." She said as she did a spin.

"No I love it." He said as he walked over to her.

He kissed her as he cupped her cheek. He rubbed his nose against hers which made her smile. But he could still see the fear and guilt in her eyes.

"Come on baby." He whispered

They sat down on the floor where he made them a spot as Roberta Flack's The First Time I Ever Saw Your Face played through his Alexa speaker. They began to drink the champagne and he fed her strawberries as she fed him.

When they finished the strawberries they began make out as he laid her down. As the make out session began to get steamier clothes began to come off. Jammy pushed his way into her as he kissed her with open mouth kisses. He wrapped one of her legs as he dug deep into her. He moved to her neck.

"James!" She cried out as she arched.

He let out a small grunt. "McKenna." He whispered as he slid one of his hands into hers above her head.

He rolled them to where she was on top and she began to ride him.

"Oh God yes! Mmm fuck me baby." He whispered as she ran her finger nails down his chest.

She began to ride him hard as he kept massaging her breasts. He raised up to her and kissed her.

"Mmm James! James!" She cried out as she reared her head back.

"That's it baby come all over my dick." He whispered as he laid her back down he wrapped both of her legs and kissed her as he began to move.

"I love the way you scream my name." He said as he held both of hands.

He began to move faster and faster. "Oh James! Right there!" She cried out

"Oh god yeah. Baby I'm right there with you. MCKENNA! MCKENNA!" He cried out as he filled her with his.

He collapsed beside her on the floor. All that was heard was the fire cracklings from the fire place. After a few minutes of silence he looked over at her he kissed her hand.

She looked over at him. "Im ready to leave her." He whispered

"James.." she whispered

"No not because of that. She doesn't love me anymore I can tell. She wants nothing to do with me. For the last 3 and half years she changed. It's either she doesn't love me or my devil of a father has turned her against me. It doesn't matter what the reasoning is for her being so cold towards me." He said as he rolled over to her as he adjusted the sheet.

"Why did you call him that?" She whispered

"Because he's a horrible ass..and a abuser and so many other things. But he hates me." He said

"Don't say that. Parents aren't supposed to hate their children.."

"Well it's true. I'm the reason why my parents are divorced. When I was 12 I found my dad in bed with his 22 year old secretary. I called my mom all upset and crying she came home. They yelled for hours till my mom kicked him out." He said as he played with her hair.

"When he left he said good bye to all of us. When he got to me he backhanded me hard across the face. He told me I needed to learn to mind my business and keep my mouth shut. And the abuse didn't stop there. He continued to take his anger out on me. I had a black eye in my mom's wedding photos. He hates me..I didn't tell anyone I bottled it up and found other ways to deal with it all. Till I crashes my car at 17 and almost died. That's how I met Lucas we met at one of those drug meetings. We help each other fight old urges. I met Shayla shortly after I got better. She doesn't know any of this." He said

She cupped his cheek, hearing his story broke her heart.

"What about you?" He said

"What about me?" She said

"I'm no idiot. You are very beautiful I was surprised there was no ring on this hand. And you are very guarded." He said

She propped herself up on her elbow. "I had a fiancé. But we broke up four years ago." She said

"Cold feet?" He said

"No..I broke it off cause he was being a insensitive prick. I had just lost my dad, given the bakery and guardianship of my little sister. And he was more concerned about himself." She said

"What happened to your dad?" He said

"He had a massive stroke and he never woke up." She said

"And your mom?" He said

"You don't know." She said as a tear fell.

"Know what?" He said as he propped himself up on his elbow.

"She was killed when I was 9. A robber tried to rob her at gunpoint as she was leaving the bakery late one night. She had the deposit bag she wouldn't let him have it. So he shot her twice. I thought everyone knew it was all over the news and papers." She said

He wiped her tears and rested his forehead against hers. "I'm so sorry." He whispered as he kissed her.

She looked at him and kissed him. "Happy New Year." He said

"Happy New Year." He said as he kissed her and laid her back down.

(13) Celebrations & Truths Unraveled

Three weeks later

"Why would your mom invite that man?" Lucas said

"Same reason she invited him to the wedding. He's my father. And this is his parents house." Jammy said

Winnie and her ex in laws threw a party to celebrate his company's first international client. He had been gaining momentum all over the US. Now he's got his first building going up in Sydney. The party was the last place he wanted to be he rather be at McKenna's or have McKenna with him.

James tried to talk Jammy but he just walked off from him. He went to get some air on the back porch and puff on his cigar. Lucas went to go find a bathroom he made his way through the crowd of people that were friends and family of Jammy's. All the other bathrooms were occupied so he went upstairs.

As he was coming back down the hall after taking a leak. He heard noises from a bedroom the sounds of sex.

"Who the hell is treating this like it's highschool." He said to himself

He peaked through a small crack to see his best friend's wife on top of her father in law riding him like nobody's business.

He leaned against the wall. "Oh my god Jam will lose his shit." He thought

He quickly made his way downstairs, he found Jammy. "Hey man I gotta go. I'll see you tomorrow okay." He said

"You alright.." Jammy said

"Yeah I'm good." He said

Lucas made his way back into the party found the others to tell them to meet him tomorrow at Jammy's tomorrow. He left the party and drove to his older sister's house. His brother in law Shannon worked for James.

They went into Shannon's home office. "What's wrong?" He said

"Did you know that James' dad was sleeping with his wife?" Lucas said

"Who is James' wife?" Shannon said

"Shayla..Shayla Barnes." He said

"You mean the office slut. She is sleeping with everyone there not just her father in law. I'm the only one who stays away from that mess. He uses her as a way to get deals done." Shannon said

"I need you to come with me tomorrow." Lucas said

"Okay." Shannon said

****

"Hey everyone." Jammy said as he let everyone in.

Lucas came in last with Shannon on his tail. "This is my brother in law Shannon. I brought him here and asked everyone to come cause we are going to need some help." Lucas said

"Okay." Jammy said

Once everyone was seated. "Last night the reason I bolted the party was because I found your dad and Shayla in bed having sex at the party." Lucas said

Jammy's mouth fell open.

"Shannon works for your dad. He knows more.." Lucas said

"I'm sorry James. She's been dubbed the office slut..she's been sleeping with your dad but she's also having relations with other colleagues. I wouldn't be surprised if when they say she knows how to close a deal for James that she's fucking them. I stay far the hell away from all that." Shannon said

Jiovanni calls their other brother Marcelo who lives in London. "That dirty fucking no good two timing bitch." He said

Marcelo answered the phone. "Hey brother." He said

Jiovanni tells him to find whatever he can on the two of them. While Sam calls his sister who is a divorce lawyer to help Jammy file for divorce. Jammy stood up and walked over to where they had their wedding photos and threw them against the wall and left.

(14) The Unraveling

Three days later

Jammy was standing in his office just staring out his big glass window. It was snowing in NY as cars drove by. His two stepbrothers and Lucas came into the office.

"Hey James, you alright?" Jio said

"Oh hey guys.." he said as he turned around and walked towards his desk.

"We have been trying to check on you the last few days but there was no answer at the penthouse. And your door man said he hasn't seen you." Lucas said

"That's because I've been staying at McKenna's." He said as he sat down.

"So Marcelo's flight from London lands at 2PM. Me and Malcolm will pick him up. So where do you want to meet? The penthouse? Mine and Malcolm's place? Here or McKenna's" Jio said

"Not McKenna's. I don't want to drag Mckenna into this." He said

"Drag me into what?" McKenna said as she came in.

She had brought him lunch from his favorite Italian place in Brooklyn. She was in the city to go to her eye appointment and to get her birth control pills. He took his food from her and kissed her. The three men were shocked by the kiss as they looked at each other.

"You don't want to drag me into what James?" She said

"Our brother Marcelo have more info on Shayla's infidelity. We were just discussing where to meet." Malcolm said

"Oh, well if you need to use my apartment you can. Nobody is allowed up there but me or my little sis-." She said but was cut off.

"No Mckenna. I just said no I don't want you dragged into it." Jammy snapped

McKenna swallowed hard and looked at her phone. "I'm gonna go so I'm not late." She said

She walked out, "Dude we know you are stressed and ball of emotions right now. But snapping at her wasn't the way to be." Lucas said

Jammy looked down as he left to catch up to her. He found her waiting at the elevator.

"Kenna baby. I'm not trying to be a dick. I just don't want you dragged in there is no telling what they have found. I know my father he will do anything for a deal. And get involved with the wrong people. So I'm sorry for snapping." He said

"I just wanted to be there for you James. But I have to go before I'm late." She said as she stepped into the elevator.

"McKenna baby don't leave upset." He said

When the doors closed he sighed. "I'm just trying to protect you." He whispered as he walked away.

McKenna ignored him the rest of the day. She got her new contacts and birth control before heading home to Brooklyn. The boys all met at Jio and Malcolm's place. Jammy continued to get McKenna to answer him but she just kept leaving his messages on read.

"Okay well let's start with some easier things to digest. Your father has several illegitimate children including an a 19 year old. But there is this with your wife James, a still born baby girl who would have been two this June." Marcelo said

Jammy read the birth certificate and death certificate. "We were in Seattle. That's when we had our first building go up outside of NY. She never looked or acted pregnant." Jammy said

"Oh but she was. Here's all of the medical records. According to bank statements there is a lot trips to beach vacations. Not just business trips. It looks like this has been going on for three and half years too." Marcelo said

"How can you tell that?" Sam said

"Because this is the first many videos I've found. I was able to get in contact with his security guy and pretended to be a member of the BBB (Better Business Bureau) and was able to obtain a lot of CCTV." Marcelo said

He press play its James' conference room and Shayla on all fours with James behind her the potential client being sucked off. In the middle of the table as they discussed their business deal. In another video on the same disc was Shayla having sex in the middle of the table with James. She was riding him just like Lucas found them she was riding him like nobody's business and James was enjoying every bit of it. More clips followed of the other office slut and her being bent over the table and the other employees getting their rocks off.

Marcelo turned it off, he looked at his brothers. "What?" Jio said

"Just be prepared all of you. This next clip on this disc is very vile." He said

He pressed play there was all kinds of naked people on the screen in a hotel room and lots of sex noises.

"That's the Bertoli's and some of my old friends from London." Jiovanni said

"Well now I know why Xavier and Salvatore quit talking to me at the office." Shannon said

Jammy walked out on the balcony to get some air. Lucas followed him, "A fucking orgy Luke! My father had my wife turn against me. She gave birth to my sister! Do you know how disgusting that sounds! He was fucking my wife and letting everyone else screw her too.!" Jammy said as he began to pace.

"I know.." Lucas said

He gave Jammy a few more minutes to calm down before they went back inside.

"Sam..tell your sister that we signed a prenup and that Shayla Ann Reynolds isn't getting fucking dime of my money. She isn't getting shit from me! And I want the divorce papers to her like yesterday." Jammy said as he left.

Once he parked by McKenna's car behind the bakery he had calm down. He let himself in with his key. All the lights were off but Mckenna was awake as she laid in bed. Jammy slipped off his shoes and undid his tie. As she heard him throw his wallet watch phone and keys on the night stand. She sat up as he was unbuttoning his shirt.

"Is because I'm the mistress?" She said

"What?" He said confused

She crawled over to his side of the bed and stood on her knees. "Earlier, is it because I'm the other woman?" She said

He held her hips after he took off his shirt. "You are not the mistress or the other woman. You are the woman I am falling in love with. The woman that calms me down and keeps me sane. The woman that I love. You are nothing less..I wasn't trying to be an ass I just didn't know what I was about to find out. You should be happy that you weren't there. But right now I need to show you just how much I love you Mckenna Grace." He said as he dropped his pants and boxers.

After they were done he told her what all was unraveled. It made her want to throw up.

(15) MOVING OUT & ON

A week later

Jammy had his sleeves rolled up as he stood behind Mckenna in the bakery kitchen. They were making apple turnovers together. Once they were done they took them upstairs to her apartment. They cooled while they made dinner together and danced in the kitchen.

Once they had dinner and dessert they enjoyed a hot bath in her claw foot tub with bubbles.

"I got the new penthouse." He said as they sat in the tub.

"You're leaving me?" She said as she looked up at him

"I'm not leaving you. I told you that I love you and I understand that you aren't ready to say it back. But you can always move in with me" he said as he put his chin on her shoulder as he wrapped his arms around her.

"James.." she whispered

"What?" He whispered

"Let's sleep naked I like when we do that." She said

"You mean let's have sex till we fall asleep cause I like when we do that too." He whispered as he let go of her.

The next day he was looking around his new place with McKenna. When Winnie called him.

"Hey mom." He said

"Hey sweetie, I was just calling to check on you. You have been distant the last week or so." Winnie said

"I know mom. I've had a lot of shit going on..I um I will explain more in person once everything is done. But me and Shayla are going our separate ways." He said as he sat on the stairs.

"Honey..what happened?" Winnie said

"I'll explain more later mom. I just it's not something you say over the phone. Just know that it's all okay." He said

"Okay sweetie. I love you baby." She said

"I love you mama." He said and hung up.

McKenna sat beside him. "I like your kitchen." She said as he took her hand and she laid her head on his shoulder.

He kissed her head. "I like all of it. The only part I don't like is the fact that I'm no longer across the street from you. Or not having you in my bed." He said

She kissed him. "Who says that I won't be. Just because I said no to moving in together didn't mean I wasn't going to stay with you some nights." She said

"I know." He said as he caressed her cheek.

(16) Breaking News!!

Two weeks later

Shayla came home to see the penthouse was trashed. Their wedding photos broken.

"Jammy?" She said

She went into his home office to find it completely empty.

"No..Jammy!" She said as she ran to the bedroom.

All of his clothes was gone his closet was completely cleaned out. She tried to call and text him to get no answer. She grabbed her keys and drove over to James' place. Since she had a key she let herself in.

"James!" She yelled as she went upstairs.

She kicked the door open to find a blonde on top of him. "Get out." She said as she pulled the girl off by her hair.

"Shayla baby. What is the matter?" James said

"You told him didn't you? You told James about us?" She said

"I haven't told anyone." He said

"He's gone. He's left me all of his stuff is gone." She said

The girl came back in to get her shoes. "Good luck you two." She said and walked out.

James looked at her the blonde confused. "Let's just go to work okay?" He said

They went to the office where there was reporters standing outside.

"What the hell is going on?" James said

They went inside and up to his office. James turned on the tv just as another person walked into the office.

"Mrs Shayla Ann Barnes you've been served." The guy said

She opened the blue envelope to reveal divorce papers already signed.

"This just in..it appears the source is someone trying to get to the Bertoli's. But James Barnes the CEO of Barnes Engineering has been labeled a womanizer, and has been having relations with his daughter in law Shayla Ann Reynolds-Barnes. She's married to Mr Barnes youngest son James Barnes III the CEO of BRW Contracting and Engineering. She's also the heiress of Reynolds Inc.."

James threw the remote into the tv. "That fucking bastard son of mine. He did this I know it was him." James yelled as the mail person came in.

"Mrs Barnes.." he said as he hands her a Manila envelope.

She opened up to see pictures and the baby's death and birth certificates. Also inside was a note that simply said.

"Told you not to take that job. I hope you enjoy your life with him."

Shayla stood there in shock as James left. He had his driver take him to BRW when he was met by his younger brother and several security officers.

"Where is that little rat?!" James said

"You aren't allowed to be here big brother. And he isn't even here.. he's on vacation." He said as the officers escorted him.

"I'll get that little bastard when he gets back." He yelled

Jammy and McKenna was enjoying a nice beach vacation in Grenada at a Sandals resort. They were making out in a private area of the beach with her on top of him.

"You are going to make me take you right here on this towel if you don't stop." He whispered

"We could just go back to the house." She whispered.

"Mmm better idea baby doll." He said as they got up.

She jumped on his back and he carried her like that to their beach house.

(17) Discussions, Divorce and Denials

The next day after nobody answering their phones. Shayla drove over to Steve's place when Lucas answered the door.

"Luke you know him better than anyone..where is he?" She said

Lucas slammed the door in her face. She walked away with her head down, she drove off and over to Wanda's place.

Wanda answered the door.

"What the hell are you doing here?" Wanda said

"To um talk." Shayla said as she shifts her weight.

Wanda rolled her eyes and crosses her arms. "There's nothing to talk about."

The other girls make their way to the door.

"Hey Wan whose at the door...oh it's you." Nat said

"Oh hell naw." Milena said

"What the hell do you want?" Bobbi said

"Umm none of you have been answering your phones or messages." She said

"Well that sounds familiar doesn't it ladies." Wanda said

They all nod.

"I know I'm sorry but I've been busy." Shayla said

"Busy sucking dicks, having trains ran on you..being fucked by every guy in the world. Having an affair with the man that your soon to be ex husband hates. And having his baby! You are disgusting Shayla." Natasha said

"You think we want to be friends with you after all you've done to Jammy. Hell no!" Bobbi said

Shayla looked down.

"It's one thing to be a shitty friend to us. But what you did to Jammy was low as shit. All he's ever done is love you Shay. He asked you to not take that job we all may not understand the story behind his hate for James but you were his wife and should of respected his wishes." Hope said

"You treated him like shit! Rejecting him ignoring him you have no idea how much it hurts us as his friends to watch him wonder what the fuck he was doing wrong! And all while Shayla Ann was getting her vagina pounded by sixty year old men and their 20 something year old sons. We thought you had more class Shayla." Wanda said

"You had a gold mine Shay. He's loyal sexy AF and a romantic. I wish Clint does half the shit he did for you. Women would drop their panties for half the shit he did for you. And all you did was reject him time after time. You aren't worth the jail time that I would get for kicking your ass Shayla. But I would do it in a heart beat cause he is my friend." Bobbi said

"You knew the relationship with his father and you still took the job. I remember Sam telling me that three days into your marriage he was back at the apartment he use to share with Lucas. All because you two got into about the job. You are a selfish slutty bitch and I hope you get what you deserve one day." Milena said

"So our friendship is severed lose our numbers and get some help." Wanda said

"Deuces." Milena said

Natasha slammed the door and they went back to their movie A Summer Romance.

****

After she left the girls in tears, she headed to her parents. When she pulled in she saw her grandparents cars.

"Mom dad. I'm here." Shayla yelled as she went inside.

"In the kitchen." Shelia yelled (her mother)

When she goes into the kitchen her grandparents looked at her and turned back around.

"Shay what are you doing here? You haven't answered your phone or our messages for weeks. Now you just pop up out of nowhere." Preston said (her father)

"I know. I just..I don't know embarrassed." She said

"Embarrassed? You are the one who had this wonderful loving husband. Who loved you and clearly that wasn't enough." Maxine said (her grandmother)

"Shay what the hell were you thinking? Not only did you embarrass our family and his. You completely humiliated that boy. Did I not give you enough love or attention growing up? Cause I honestly don't know what would possess you to go after his father." Preston said

Shayla began to cry. "No daddy that wasn't it." She said

"Then what in God's green earth would make you sleep with your father in law?" Shelia said

Shayla sniffled. "James..I mean Mr Barnes and I were working late one night and he came on to me. Me and James were having problems we hadn't had sex in awhile and fighting a lot. So I gave in. It was only suppose to be a one time thing but I couldn't stop thinking about how good it felt. So we started to have sex more often." She said

"How long.." Preston said

"3 and half years.." she said

"Jesus Christ..that's almost your whole entire marriage." Shelia said

"Is the reason why you went missing at the gala and the party that his mother threw for him." Shelia said

Shayla shook her head yes.

"My God Shayla Ann!" Preston said as he threw his napkin on the table.

"Was he also the reason why you avoided baby talk with little James?" Mason said (her grandfather)

"Yes and no." She said

"What does that mean?" Maxine said

She bit her lip and looked down.

"Shayla answer your grandmother." Preston said in a stern tone.

"It means I had a baby..that was Ja- Mr Barnes..at the time that Jammy was pushing the conversation I was pregnant. I had a baby girl but she died." Shayla said

"Shayla Ann Reynolds!!" Preston said as he stood up.

Suddenly she was the only one left in the kitchen. Her grandparents left to try and salvage the friendship the families had. And her parents couldn't look at her so she left.

****

It was the morning of the divorce hearing two days later. She seen Jammy waiting outside the court room.

"Jammy please don't go through with this." She said

"I don't know who you are anymore. I don't love you anymore I can never look at you the same way again Shayla. And the only reason why you are doing this now is because that SOB dropped your ass to the curb. Go back to him Shayla or who ever else there was. But I'm through with you and this marriage. You gave birth to my sister that alone makes me want to throw up." He said as he walked off.

She ran to the bathroom to throw up and cry till it was time to go in. By the end of the hearing Jammy walked out with his money his business and left Shayla in the dust. That afternoon Shayla found out through a pee stick she was pregnant again. But James denied it was his and told her to leave his apartment.

(18) I'm All Yours

Three months later

"Hey you." Jammy said as he kissed McKenna's neck.

"Hey." She said

"I have good news." He said as they sway as she made them supper in his kitchen.

"Mm what is that?" She said

"I'm officially all yours baby." He whispered as he sucked on her neck.

She giggled. "James oh gosh James..I'm..trying to cook you dinner." She whispered as she felt his hand down her pants.

"I prefer dinner in bed." He whispered as he turned off the burner. He threw her over his shoulder and smacked her ass.

"James!" She yelped as he carried her upstairs.

Once they made it to his bedroom. "You don't need any of these things." He said as he stripped her down.

He laid her down on the bed and lowered in between her legs. He began to devour her and left beard burn and bite marks. McKenna was seeing stars she didn't even notice when he began to have his way with her by sex.

"It's all yours baby. I love you Mckenna Grace Harlow. You are mine." He said in her ear as he filled her with his juices.

She looked at him. "You..I..love you too." She said as she kissed him.

He smiled at her. "We don't have to hide anymore baby. And I already know that my mama is going to love you." He said

She rolled to her side and kissed him. "Now will you please move in with me?" He said

She looked down. "Baby what are you so scared of?" He said

"The last time I moved in with a boyfriend it didn't end well James." She whispered

Jammy lifted her chin. "We can wait till your ready. But one of the main reasons why I want you here with me. Is because you living above your bakery isn't safe baby. One accidental fire that starts in your kitchen in the bakery and the whole building could go up in flames. Leaving struggling to get out." He said

"I love you James now I'm going to go finish making dinner." She said

"I've already had my dinner." He said

She gasped. "I'm playing..come on I'll help." He said

(19) Slap Fest

The next day

"Hey sweetie." Winnie said as Jammy came in.

"Hey mom." He said

"You brought me dessert." She said

"I did. You said you were making lunch". He said

"Come on I made sure everyone was gone so we can talk." She said

They went into the sunroom and sat down.

"So tell me baby. How did you find out?" She said as she grabbed his hand and squeezed it.

"The night of our big celebration. Lucas bolted the party acting weird the next day he came over with his brother in law. He told me he left because he found...that man and her in bed. Shannon began to tell me that she was dubbed the office slut. Marcelo found out about the disgusting vile things he made her do. She had a baby with him mom she had my sister. And dad has other children did you know that. Dad has other kids he doesn't claim including one with that bitch I found him with all those years ago." He said

"I know baby. Your father is a sick man. But I am so happy that you got yourself out of this mess." She said

He smiled at her. "Well there is something else I need to tell you. And I don't want you to get upset. But I've been spending a lot of time with someone new. She's amazing and just so you know three weeks before I found all this out we started sleeping together. I'm in love with her..she is amazing mom." He said

"Honey..I don't blame you for looking for the love and the affection that you weren't getting from that woman. And I can't wait to meet this girl that has brought this smile on." She said as she caressed his cheek.

"Well you kinda already have." He said

She looked at him confused. He tapped the top of the cake box he brought in. "McKenna is the girl I've been seeing mom." He said

She gasped. "Oh baby! That makes me so excited! I love her and I always thought you two would be so cute together when I would see her by her mama's side watching her every move. She's beautiful baby. And when you bring her over have her bring me one of these." She said as she opened the cake.

As they were continuing the conversation. They heard

"Winnie!! Where are you?"

She went inside as she told Jammy to stay put.

"You cant just walk in my house!" She said

"I'll do what I Damn well please woman. Give me that little snitch! He's the reason why my business has tanked." James said

Winnie hauled off and smacked him hard. "You get the hell out of my house! You brought this all on your self James Buchanan Barnes II. Don't you blame my son for any of it! Now leave before I call the cops for breaking and entering! You stay away from my kids!" Winnie yelled

"Not until I talk to him. I know he is that's his car in the driveway." James said

Jammy slammed his napkin on the table. "Get the hell out of mom's house! You aren't her husband you are nothing to mom! So fucking leave!" Jammy said as he came inside.

"Ah there he is. Done hiding behind your mama." James said as he came for Jammy.

He went to smack him when Jammy blocked him and punched him hard in the nose. Knocking James on to the ground. Giving Winnie plenty enough of time to call the cops. They arrested James and escorted him out.

Later that day after Jammy left Shayla showed up to apologize. Before she could even say anything Winnie smacked her hard across the face.

"You better never show your face here again. I'll tell you the same thing I told your family. There will be no reconciliation. Because everytime that I would look at you I will be reminded that not only did you hurt my son but you also slept with my ex husband and had his baby. Had threesomes." Winnie said

Shayla looked down.

"So leave my premises cause I would hate to have to call the cops again." She said

Shayla walked out with her head hung low.

(20) Meeting the Family

Two weeks later

Jammy woke up alone in his bed. "Kenna baby." He whispered.

He didn't see her anywhere in his apartment he found his phone.

"Hello.." she said

"Where are you baby?" He said

"Um, well I'm at the bakery. I'm making pies and cakes for us to go meet your family later." She said

"McKenna baby you don't have to go all out." He said

She rolled her eyes.

"Mom already loves you. And the rest of them are going to love you." He said as he pulled on clothes.

"I have to mix this lemon cake James." She said

"I'll be there soon." He said as he hung up.

He came through the back to see her decorating a strawberry cake. He went to make a cup of coffee and came over to her. When she looked at him she was red and sweaty.

"Baby please stop. You are hot and sweating trying to make cakes and pies." He said

"Well I also made all the breakfast stuff that has been put out too." She said

He pulled her over to him to stand in between his legs. He pushed some of her blonde hair out of her face.

"You are doing to much. You need to slow down." He said

She finished her cakes and baked the last pie before heading upstairs to get ready.

****

When they pulled into his mom's driveway she was amazed by how big the house was.

"What's with the face?" He said

"I just the house is huge." She said

"Well you are about to find out why." He said

He opened the door for her and got all the cakes and pies out of the backseat. They walked up to the door. Winnie opened it before the got to it.

She told the two maids behind her to take the boxes to the kitchen.

"McKenna this is my mom Winnie, Mom this is Mckenna." Jammy said

Winnie smiled. "I know who she is James. But it's nice to finally be formally introduced." Winnie said as she led them into the sitting room.

Jammy took a deep breathe, "McKenna darlin, this is my family. My step dad Marcus, his kids Marcelo is who you haven't met he's the oldest. You already met Jiovanni and Malcolm. Their sister Janessa and her husband Jaquez. Over there is my brother Elijah and his wife, my brother Jasper and his wife. My sisters Rebecca Ruthie and Odette and their husbands. And of course all of mom's grandbabies are in the playroom." He said

"Wow.." she whispered

"Everyone this is Mckenna Harlow. My girlfriend." He said

"Now I understand the big house." She whispered as they all went into the dining room to eat.

"Yup. Mom married him when I was 15 Marcelo and Elijah were the only two off at college." He said

They all enjoyed the dessert when it came time for the cakes and the pies she had made. Jammy noticed that she was starting become quieter as the night went on. On the way home he looked at her.

"Baby what's wrong?" He said

"It's nothing really. Just being around your family today just really made me miss my parents. I wish I could do what you did today. Take you over for dinner you can't have dinner with dead people." She said

"I remember your parents. I seen them all the time at the bakery. They were two beautiful people so in love." He said as they turned into his building's parking garage.

When they were sitting in the tub he wrapped his arms around her. "I love you my darling." He whispered

She smiled. "I love you too." She whispered

(21) McKenna's Surprise Party

Six months later

It was October 5th Alexis and Melinda both had to keep McKenna away from the bakery. It was her 29th birthday. Jammy with the help of Rochelle and Lucas planned a surprise birthday party.

It was finally time for the party where everyone was waiting in the dark of the bakery. The girls snuck her in through the back. Alexis kept her hands over her eyes till they were in the front. She took her hands off and Mel hit the lights.

"SURPRISE!!!!"

She jumped when she heard everyone and she saw her whole bakery filled with friends and family. Jammy came over to her and kissed her.

"Happy birthday." He said

"Thank you." She said with a smile.

"Welcome." He said

They all mingled for awhile and enjoyed the party. Jammy nodded to Lucas who looked to Rochelle. She stood in the middle of the room.

"Can I have everyone's attention. We need everyone to take a spot that isn't here. We need the birthday girl." Rochelle said

McKenna walked over to her. "Okay you stay here. And don't turn around till we say so." Rochelle said as Makayla walked out with one of the bakeries pink boxes.

She opened the box and Rochelle pointed to the letter on the lid.

"Remember the day we met, because of I was running late and the donuts were wrong. Lift up the paper to see if the donuts are still wrong."

She was confused so she left the parchment paper. Inside was pink and green glazed donuts just like that day. She gasped when she read what they were spelling out. "WILL YOU MARRY ME?"

She turned around and saw Jammy down on one knee with the ring box open. Tears fell as she shook her head yes. He slid the ring on her finger as he stood up. He kissed her.

"I love you baby." He whispered

"I love you too. You did this all for me." She whispered

"I had a little help." He said as he nodded towards Lucas and Rochelle making faces at each other.

She kissed him. "Thank you for making this the best birthday." She said

"Oh believe me baby. I will continue to make your birthday the best day ever. It's the most special day of all. It's the day that the woman I love came into this world." He whispered as he picked her up and kissed her.

(22) The New Mrs Barnes

Eight months later

On June 20th family and friends were gathered in a ballroom at the Hilton hotel.

Raegan pulled McKenna's veil down. "Thank you Rae." She whispered

"Anytime." She said

McKenna swallowed back the lump in her throat.

"Raegan I'll see you down there." Gabe said as he kissed her cheek and placed his hand on her growing baby bump.

He came around to face his sister. "I can't believe I have to do this twice this year you and Gracie have grown into two beautiful women.

Dad and mom are smiling down today. Although mom would be mad at you for making your own wedding cake." He said

She let out a laugh. "We did it Mckenna. We made it together like we always have. Now it's all three of us building our own families. Granted I got a head start." He said

"You always have." She said

"I am the oldest. But I've had the best partner in crime in my little sister." He said

"Yeah." She said

"So let's get you to your groom." He said as he held out his arm.

She linked her arm with her brother's and they went downstairs. Lucas was the best man and Rochelle was her maid of honor. They had her niece be the flower girl and Jammy's nephew be the ring bearer.

Jammy smiled so big when the doors open he felt his heart skip a beat just like the first time he ever met her.

"Who gives this woman to this man?" The minster said

"I Gabriel Harlow in honor of our late parents Bryant and Melissa Harlow." Gabe said

He kissed her cheek than sat down.

The ceremony continued with the minister reading from the Bible and going on about love and marriage. It was finally time for the vows.

"James, from the moment we met that day you made me have butterflies. That hasn't changed you have continued to do so. You keep me sane you keep me reminding me how much I mean to you. I love the way we can talk for hours the way you surprise me with romantic dinners. You are the love that I always wanted. I'll never understand what you saw me but I don't regret it. You are the love of my life and I'm so thankful that you never gave up.I can't wait to start building our future together to have babies and love you till..till death do us apart." She said

"McKenna, from the moment we met I was drawn to you. I couldn't get you out of my mind you helped me through so much. Sometimes all it took was a simple smile from you to remind myself to get out of my head. You are an amazing talented smart independent and sometimes a little stubborn. But you are the woman I love the woman I was meant to find and give my heart to. The woman that is everything to me. And like I always have told you,you much more than what you think you are. Cause to me you are the world baby my world. I love you Mckenna." He said

They exchanged their rings and ended the ceremony with a kiss where Jammy dipped her and kissed her.

They shared their first dance together to "To Make You Feel My Love" the Adele version.

(23) Cayman Islands

That night they left for the Cayman Islands, for their week long honeymoon. They left on Jammy's private jet just like all the other trips. Jammy and her had sex on the plane in the bedroom area of the jet.

When they landed they got a rental car and left the airport for their beach house. They fell asleep as soon as they hit the bed. The next morning they enjoyed breakfast with a gorgeous view of the beach. They went parasailing together and deep sea fishing too.

By day three of their honeymoon they went scuba diving, jet skiing and kayaking. On their last night in the Caymans. They enjoyed a romantic dinner on the beach and a hot stone couples massage. When they returned to their house just like all the other nights they had mad passionate sex together.

****

Six weeks later

"Baby you alright?" He said when he woke up to puking sounds.

He sat down beside her and rubbed her back.

"I think you are pregnant. Cause you haven't had your period since we got back from our honeymoon baby." He said

She looked at him as she wiped her mouth. "Get me a test." She said as she laid in the floor.

"Okay." He said with a smile.

When he returned from the pharmacy he gave her some ginger ale and the test. She drank some of the ginger ale. Jammy left her to do her business, he sat down on the bed as he waited. Two minutes later McKenna emerged.

She smiled at him as she tapped the test against her hand.

"It appears that you have added another family role to your name. You are not just a son brother friend and husband...you are now a daddy." She said

"You're pregnant baby!" He said as he picked her up and spun her.

They shared a kiss as she wrapped her legs around his waist.

(24) Meet Henry James Barnes

It was three in the morning on Jammy's birthday March 10th. He and McKenna had just arrived at the hospital. She had been having contractions for two hours and they came in when they got closer together.

Her doctor checked her cervix when she came in. "Oh yeah we are ready to go Mrs Barnes." She said

Jammy made the phone calls to the family and to their friends. While McKenna was getting her epidural done. He laid down beside her on the bed and held her hand and the sound of their son's heart beat lulled them both to sleep. The nurse's periodically came in and checked her cervix.

After five hours of being there it was finally time to push. After four pushed at 835 AM their son Henry James Barnes was born. He was 8lbs and 7oz and 20 inches long. Dark hair and big blue eyes. Winnie was over the moon when Jammy placed him in her arms.

"Here we go again." Elijah said in a low tone

"Shush." Winnie said not taking her eyes off her newest grandson.

"Mama's favorite gave her a new grandson." Jasper said

"I love all my children the same Jasper James. But he is my baby boy my last boy no different than Odette is my baby girl cause she is the last one of my girls." Winnie said

"I'm the last one period. And now this little nephew of mine not only shares a birthday with his daddy he shares one with his favorite auntie." Odette said

"You don't know that he can't talk yet." Ruthie said

"Oh I know. " she said as she took Henry and sat down with him.

Winnie cut her older children a look. She knew why they felt that Jammy was the favorite of the six cause he was the one that told her about James' cheating.

"Well I'm out. Congrats James." Elijah said as him and Jasper left.

Winnie hugged Jammy and McKenna as the others gushed.

EPILOGUE

The Barnes: Jammy and McKenna went on to have two more kids. They had second son when Henry was two years old. They named him Bryson James Barnes. When he was three and Henry was 5 they completed their family with a baby girl "Sage Harlow Barnes."

Both businesses continued to thrive, Jammy as a surprise wedding gift to Mckenna. He had his company redo the whole top floor of the bakery. He turned it into her wedding cake work space. She had a brand new office up there and a place to have couples do wedding cake tastings. Bryson and Henry took over Jammy's business while Sage took over the bakery.

****

Lucas and Rochelle: Got married a year after Jammy and McKenna. They had two boys and two girls. Both boys joined Bryson and Henry at BRW. Their girls followed their mama's foot steps in keeping her salon running.

****

Jio and Melinda: Had three babies together all three were boys. They lived together but never got married. They didn't see the point considering they felt it was just a piece of paper.

I***********************

Malcolm and Alexis: Did get married had three kids. Two girls and a boy.

****

Shayla and James: After a paternity test determined that Shayla's twins were in fact James' and she told him she never let any of them release inside her. She moved in with him and they never got married but had three more kids together. Jammy never claimed them as family it made him sick that his ex wife was having babies with his "sperm donor."

****

Marcelo: He moved to NY after meeting a woman when he visited. They had kids of their own and married. They lived in upstate NY.

www.ingramcontent.com/pod-product-compliance
Lightning Source LLC
Chambersburg PA
CBHW071021080526
44587CB00015B/2446